City Nave

Poems

BETSY K. BROWN

RESOURCE *Publications* · Eugene, Oregon

CITY NAVE
Poems

Resource Publications
An Imprint of Wipf and Stock Publishers
199 W. 8th Ave., Suite 3
Eugene, OR 97401

www.wipfandstock.com

PAPERBACK ISBN: 979-8-3852-1399-3
HARDCOVER ISBN: 979-8-3852-1400-6
EBOOK ISBN: 979-8-3852-1401-3

05/08/24

"The poems in *City Nave* twist and slither off the page, never still, ablaze one breath and ashen the next, here admonishing, there searching, always, like a Phoenix, fiery, always re-birthing."

—**MISCHA WILLETT,**
author of *The Elegy Beta*

"This poetry collection by Betsy K. Brown is something worth sitting up and noticing. Brown writes poems with an easy, contemporary sensibility that's like chatting with someone you know and like. But wait a second! There's something more. Formal structures and old ways, long forgotten ideas, the scent of the ruins of a civilization we once knew. A graceful and agile tone delivering tense and taut content. This is what poems are supposed to be."

—**MORGAN MEIS,**
author of *The Drunken Silenus*

"Brown's deployment of traditional forms—sonnet, shape form poems, terza rima, etc.—engages the poetic tradition both structurally and affectively, as her individual talent candidly recognizes the standards by which she would be measured. The poet consciously speaks of the poet's craft of order, insight, and surprise—with plenty of all three in *City Nave*."

—**ROBERT JACKSON,**
founder, *Classical Commons*

"Infused with the humor of a teacher who spends her days among children and the eye of a poet who finds transcendent glory and prayer all around her even in the drought-ridden desert and the suffering of a lost one, Betsy K. Brown brings a gorgeous tapestry of experience witnessed by a wise and observant eye."

—**JEANNETTE DECELLES-ZWERNEMAN,**
author of *Teaching Fiction from the Inside Out*

"Betsy K. Brown's *City Nave* is a collection of poems that span many shapes and approaches, sometimes a 'whisper / just wise / enough to feel real,' sometimes 'mariachi and trashcan drums and rap / And something that could maybe be worship.' In this synoptic collection, which conceives of the human pupil as 'the tunnel with light at both ends,' we get to witness a promising debut."

—AMIT MAJMUDAR,
author of *Twin A*

"When I met Betsy K. Brown, I had no idea, as one cannot at first, that within her was a quarrel with herself that has led her to a sublime, fierce poetry of Catholic faith—but there is. Her unsettled, intense, and thoughtful quarrel with herself plays itself out in every dimension: rhetoric, description, metrics, themes, and more."

—DAVID J. ROTHMAN,
author of *My Brother's Keeper*

"Betsy K. Brown is a poet of crisp clarity and formal jubilance. The poems in *City Nave* are all beautifully, prayerfully rooted in the details of our earthly existence and the breadth of our reach towards the transcendent. Their radiant vision moves from saints to mothers, from praise to elegy, from the wise voice of a child in the womb to contemporary psalms seeking the sacred."

—KATIE HARTSOCK,
author of *Wolf Trees: Poems*

"Betsy K. Brown's debut collection introduces a poet capable of deep love: love of the students who enter her classroom, of nature, of cities and buildings. In formal and free verse, Brown turns the clear eye of love towards the things of the world around her, revealing both their flaws and their luminous beauty so clearly that we cannot but see—and love—them too."

—J. C. SCHARL,
author of *Sonnez Les Matines*

"Betsy K. Brown's poems put flesh on the claim that art redeems life. Brown wins the world back by situating us relationally—a child from within her mother's womb, a sister in flight above the earth below, a neighbor before a broken man. Visions rise from within and from beyond—from within a tent looking out, beneath the stars, in a hummingbird's garden, among the city's forgotten places, in memory of a student who died, facing new life in a new home, praying old prayers in God's house and among his Saints. Each poem is like a beatitude, a selfless gift met by the promise of blessing."

—ANDREW J. ZWERNEMAN,
author of *History Forgotten and Remembered*

CITY NAVE

For Sam, who likes to walk through cities and churches with me

CONTENTS

ACKNOWLEDGEMENTS

THANKS BE TO GOD! And thank you to the many beloved people who together have made me a writer: the Pema family, for praying my book baby into being; my first poetry professor, Rob Jackson, for being my godfather in all things poesy and pedagogy; Tessa Carman and Jane Clark Scharl, my women who are always up to something; my undergrad and grad school folks for joining me in discovering saints, philosophers, and poets; my Arizona friends for making a longstanding local community of artists possible; my students for teaching me to die the good death; my relatives and in-laws for giving me endless lore to write about; Bolt, my first partner in making art and surviving New York; Logan, my dearest lyricist; Margi, the little sister I always look up to; Clay, who has helped me build my life; my dad for giving me grammar, guitars, and good hikes; my mom for reading with me and wondering about "the olden days;" and Sam, my editor, my husband, and my best friend.

Thanks to the editors of the following journals and sites where these poems first appeared, sometimes in slightly different versions:

Autumn Sky Poetry: "Sonnet by Those Who Stay Behind," "To a Six-Year-Old on Fifth Avenue," and "Volleyball"

The Classical Outlook: "Ode to the Original Penn Station"

Ekstasis: "Clouds," "Cursive," "Food in the Desert," "Saint John the Unfinished," "Turbulence," and "Two Ways to Be a Flame"

Fare Forward: "The Former Valley of Ashes," "Gaudete," and "Of the Baptized Apostate Hiking in Drought"

First Things: "City Nave"

The Imaginative Conservative: "The Art of Loving," "Bird, Gift," "The Lindisfarne Gospels: Saint John," "Poetry and Postulancy," and "Untangling"

The North American Anglican: "Basilique du Sacré-Coeur" and "A Young Hummingbird"

VIRTUE: "Dark Ages" and "Pupils"

Cover design: Bolt Brown

I. STAIRS

DARK AGES

The young pagans band
around the picnic table and scrawl
inky runes into their hands
with cheap pens. Around them,
the world falls, and wonders if
they will learn to rebuild it.

THE FORMER VALLEY OF ASHES, 2019

Diagonal from the strip club is a building covered in eyes.
Clear eyes crowned in turbans, the drooping eyes of
Immigrant children, eyes of dogs peering out of bags,
Eyes on every side, and two blocks down on a garage door
The green eyes of an eagle. The air here now appears clear.

The spider web of bridge is still slung over the East River;
The insect-crawl of bus and cab and train still drones; the
Storefronts still gape open in late spring. No ash farm the eye can
   see.

What blindness grows up out of this pavement now, Mr.
   Fitzgerald?
If you were here would you tell us? Would you invite us for a
   drink
Under the crystal beacons of Long Island City and tell us still that
Once we cross that bridge, anything is possible?

ODE TO THE ORIGINAL PENN STATION

A century ago, before the world
Widened, we built temples for all of our
Transitions. To catch a train to Princeton
We walked between Corinthian columns,
Sacrificing time to our steam-powered
Gods. We hurried under archways fit for
Emperors, read our papers crowned by glass
Diadems from wall to shining wall, swung
Briefcases over floors of marble. Our
Pantheon multiplied; planes arose out
Of skulls of trains; our shrines not large enough
To hold them. We wait in wide, gray cells now,
Aiming the white turbulence of our prayers
Toward bigger gods with wings that graze the sun.

BASILIQUE DU SACRÉ-COEUR

The steps of the Sacré-Coeur
billow down the hill like a robe,
and hundreds loiter on the hem, maybe
hoping to be healed. Church steps have cradled
them for centuries—the crippled, the homeless, the lost
tourists, the tired pedestrians—but here at this place are three
hundred steps instead of five or ten. The loiterers stretch on and on,
packed tight as pigeons, taking pictures, drinking lukewarm Heineken,
kissing at sunset, and all with their backs to the basilica, they face the city.
They do not turn. None of them could stand before the domes without
keeling backwards and crashing down the grime-stained steps back to
earth. So they sit upon the stone skirts, crouching toward the deep streets
of the world, held there.

FROM THE BASEMENT OF THE INTERIOR CASTLE

To the lizard I found in my closet,

I will never know just how long
You were slithering inside my clothes,
Up one cavernous sleeve and down a shirt neck,
Tunneling through pant legs, scuttling
Along seams that belong on me.

When I caught you in my water glass
I crushed your tail; it smeared
Across the calendar I slid under the cup
To carry you safely outside.
I cannot bear to kill lizards.

Is it your pleading eyes,
Red-rimmed like mine after a long night,
But wide like a child's, swearing
Up and down that you didn't know better,
Didn't mean to?

FRIENDSHIP: AN INTERLUDE

For Danny Saunders

Silence is seldom a quiet thing.
It lingers in hallways, ripe like spring
Fruit, hanging low and heavy,
Tiptoeing, shuffling, creaking.

Silence is seldom a quiet thing.
It sends sons and grandsons echoing
From ocean to ocean, street to street,
A song you can't forget how to sing.

Silence is seldom a quiet thing.
It hisses with a savage swing,
Sets spheres in motion, shatters glass,
Drawing blood, and dizzying.

Silence is seldom a quiet thing.
Restless, like textbooks, rustling,
Stacking like stones, burdens we take home,
Anxiously accumulating.

Silence is seldom a quiet thing.
Shallow, like breaths awaiting
Eye contact, a phone call, a touch
Of shoulders passing by, still there,
Silence is seldom a quiet thing.

TO A RIPE JUNE STRAWBERRY

There's a hole in the middle of your fat red heart,
And it's the first thing I notice after taking a bite.
Is this because you are not whole, Good Fruit, or
Is this to remind me that even you cannot
Satisfy me?

THIS TALE

is not new, this slow twist
   of all things into their
   almost-opposites; this whisper
      just wise
      enough to feel real,
         this true-ish toxin
            baffling our blood.
   Belly-down it binds us
   to all that we are almost meant to be.
         Lies listen to us
         so closely, so they know
      the soft pulse of skin most
      vulnerable to bite.
         We walk then with death in our veins,
            doors shut fast to the gardens
            of our hearts.
               And yet, if we look down again
               at our feet shod with shame,
               we may see what we once thought
                  was wise glistening
                  in the grasses,
                  may say, I did it,
                  may say, I may yet live,
               may stretch out, despite wounded
                  heels, and with all that is
               left of what we know is
               True, reach feet to the
               long story to crush
                  its narrow
                  head.

PHOENIX AFTER NEARBY FIRE

Flecks of once-forest settle over this city.
Red-gray shoulders slump over avenues, rest
on canals and in parking lots. I know
we must be breathing it in, bits of billows
of a ponderosa that just last year
shaded us from the sharpness of the sun.
Last week they became sun, sparked into newness
by a conflagration of car engine somewhere up the 87.

I recall the biggest bonfire we made last September.
Yuri found a brittle stump as big as an altar
and hewed it with his chainsaw, perched it aloft
on a mountain of anticipant tinder.
We set it aflame with the enthusiasm of Elijah.

The blaze became too big for roasting marshmallows,
so we sat in a wide radius ten full feet from the flame
and talked in little huddles over its roar.
We sang "I'll Fly Away" and "Swing Low" in the light
of the great caged rush of red.

SAINT MONICA

I planted my sons one by one in plots around the world
And wait like an old gardener for the rising of the dead.

Africa, Milan, New York . . .
Once or twice a year I board lonely planes
And touch down on that still-still soil,
Put my ear to the ground and grope
For my sons' growth, have a quick *how are you* cup of coffee
With one or some of them, hands clutched together quietly,
Praying another prying prayer—to God or them, I do not know.

Sometimes, when I make my way out of the tie of today
It seems they've already become saints, and I am already
Waiting in the aftermath of Rome for them to come
And send *me* home. Oh, man who will be, pray for me now.

But today is still today.
So in their dorm-cells of time they sit, and sit,
My sleeping grains of wheat, looking more
Like chaff than fruit, sons of dust, sons of tears.

I wonder if my weeping reaches far enough
Down into that ground and wets and whets
Their weary, wondering appetites, breaks through husks and
Nudges sprouts up. But I cannot ask them.

Born from my eyes I pray they rise
Soon, elbow out of the tomb, stubborn sons, squinting
With love-hate at the light, tousled young heads
Still damp with soil, still wet with watering.

OF THE BAPTIZED APOSTATE HIKING IN DROUGHT

Not even a saint could sate the tongue of
A once-wet man standing on a hill
Looking over a land where monsoon season
Never came. This man, this land, is a land where plants rattle
Like skulls' teeth, where each canyon is a dusty lung
Where trailheads gasp for want of water,
For lack of green.

This land, this man was sprinkled once,
Dunked once,
Called beloved by someone who was well-pleased.
Millions of years ago this desert was an ocean.
This mountaintop was the seashore.
I reach out a bare toe and dip it into the air.
Will I feel the water there, still?

TO MUMS

Sturdy flower,
Posture prim as a prep student's,
Not a wilting to be seen,
You crowd the tall jar with heads
Pressed calmly together, like a cat's
Against my open palm. I chose you
Because you looked most alive,
With your wine-dark petals rimmed
In frothy white, a still shot of the
Nighttime sea. Both still and moving
Are you, confident blossom,
Your tight ruffles emitting just
The slightest scent. As the hours
Go on, you will open, and I will see
More and more of your yellow eyes. O,
That the sea will never go brown
As you will, and drop its petals
Point by point
Onto the earth's hard floor!

RASKOLNIKOV IN NEW YORK CITY

Oh, what a place to all be alone together!
Today I will tape my essays to every naked pole
And hum another song of myself as I step away,
Holey shoes flapping against this relentless pavement
That presses up through my soles, presses even more
Than those old roads of Saint Petersburg.

Do not give me new clothes. Let me lean alone,
Lank and filthy against subway walls where
Once words of prophets were written till the day
They killed the songs. Now old lyrics crash together
Down here from various recesses in this tunneled
Ground, mariachi and trashcan drums and rap
And something that could maybe be worship.
I languish in its soup of what-was language and
Wonder what everyone here must think of me.

I neither come nor go; I instead loiter here from station
To station, above ground then below ground again; nowhere
Left to run from here. My bed is the corner
Somewhere near Queensborough Plaza, my
Coffin of a couch where I am left alone in the drone
Of the commuter crowd. I am still humming, humming,
Catching glimpses of ghosts of the meanderers before me,
Afraid if I look someone in the eye I might find
Something I know there, know something I find there.

SAINT JOHN THE UNFINISHED

My body is a broken temple
of the Holy spirited away
by cigarette smoke and city grime.
I grind my teeth, wanting to be washed.

The nave of my neck lies long and empty
like an abandoned subway tunnel;
the domed ceiling inside of my skull is gray and bare,
waiting to be turned into art.
But as of now, no one crosses himself before peering into me.

Shroud me in scaffolding.
I want to be wrapped up in metal poles,
white plastic, and construction workers.
Roll a stone over my whitewashed mouth.
Let me lie.
Unveil me someday.

TO MY BROTHER-IN-LAW IN KIEV FROM A PLANE OVER TEXAS

New Year's Eve, 2022

Back on earth, fireworks bloom.
As our plane takes off we see them
Toss their petals across Houston,
Red and yellow and blue and white,
Smaller than sparklers and paler than stars.
I turn on my music to settle my stomach
And watch the beauty of small bombs breaking.

It is already tomorrow in Kiev, and soon
It will be yesterday. Before the flight took
Off, Sam showed me a photo of the hotel
Near where you live, its shoulder turned
To a gaping maw of rubble and smoke.
Meanwhile tiny Texas house lights click
In rows below us like prayer beads, and
The fireworks burst and burst, so small,
In blast-beruffled plume, bewildered birds.

You texted us soon after, saying you were
Okay, sent us a picture of you with your
Friends in a bar drinking daiquiris. You, still
The same man who calls me "sis" and eggs us
On at parties, no different there than here,
Save for the rubble, save for the questions.
We toast across the Atlantic to you with
Our ginger ale and tonic water. We pray.

Everywhere people are breaking, and
Are building, and are toasting. Here's to

All the things that must break, scattering
Light like seeds from time zone to time zone,
From year to year, from life to life.

II. NARTHEX

EULOGY TO THE FIRST MS. BROWN

or *A Divine Comedy of Educators*

To my aunt—the second daughter of three,
And first to leave us just two years ago:
I picture you once sitting on Grandpa's knee

And asking him, where do our spirits go
When they leave earth? I'm sure he gave a wry
Teacher's reply to you, and that a show

Of hands shot up with questions, whys on whys,
If his students happened to hear it. That's
How it goes for us teachers—ever-wise

We aim and aim to be, as citizens cast
Us onto thrones of gold and wild guesses,
What a view! Did it ever feel too vast

To you, Aunt Lin, that map that curses, blesses
Us with endless, shining roads?
I don't know, I say again. It messes

With me, cruel doubt, and gnaws and pokes and goads—
Doubt about adding, atoms, afterlife,
Doubt about what might survive or explode—

You were a science teacher, not a wife
Or parent, but a mother all the same,
Wielding goggles and a dissecting-knife

And making children doubt and doubt again
Till lights shot up among the field of hands
And all stood, silent, staring at the flame,

The conflagration on their tiny land
Of learning, the fruit of their labors long,
A flash of something true, of something grand,

Hard to explain in lab report or song:
A consolation. Is that where you are?
I see you shining somewhere in a throng

Of light, and heat, and burning—much like a star,
But vaster. Still, the children want to know—
Is that where you are? Is that where we'll go?

THE LINDISFARNE GOSPELS: SAINT JOHN

In the beginning your fathers' fathers kidnapped heaven
And held it for ransom. Open the book,
Smell the vellum, touch the ink from the east, look
Into the labyrinthine Latin, imagine
Walking through its knotted vines and then
Emerging into a pair of eyes which look
Into you and speak in stern words: *you took*
Something that will later take you; for when
You stole this book from cloisters young,
You first exchanged it for coins and stones,
But your children's children took it back again,
Annotated its margins in their vulgar tongue,
Blessed with it their saints' and martyrs' bones,
Prayed someday the maze might let them in.

IN UTERO

My mother is the only person who
has ever fully surrounded me.
Sometimes I still float, knees to my chest,
naked, eyes bluish and barely open.
Outside noises sound plush, muffled by muscle,
tissue, fluid. I kick. I want the harsh
independence of air, the unfiltered
sounds of singing, of wind, of sirens. I
want to hurt more, to skin my knees on cracked
sidewalks, to pull splinters from my own palms.
What is this need to be birthed, to fall, to
know gravity for the first time? Again
my elbows and heels test the inner walls
of my mother. She knows what I want.
She knows my escape will take too long.
And she knows that although it is my escape,
it is her work. We wait for the divide.

TO A SIX-YEAR-OLD ON FIFTH AVENUE

The coldest winter in a hundred years.
You weave your small pink scooter through the mob
Of coats and shouts and shoppers. I chase you,
Ice in my lungs, city-din in my ears.

We watch the Christmas windows flash and dance
Like bright ballet upon your wind-burned cheeks—
Your mittened hand takes mine. You stop, entranced;

And then I turn my head. Across the street
Saint Patrick's Cathedral looms silently
And stares with unlit windows, dim and peaked.

And from our clasped hands on this crux of street
Two roads branch out—one into shadows tall,
The other into fairy-light, but both
Into the place where sound and silence meet.

FOOD IN THE DESERT

I. Mohave Connector Psalm

Lord, unsettle the dust
inside my song.
My hands are swollen
from hanging low too long.
Show me every switchback
as a palm to raise;
Show me every trail as
a throat swept with praise.

II. Wondering about My Runaway Brother

I lay on the hillside again, squinting for a glimpse of you.
The horizon slopes in a half-smile
like a teacher who knows the end of the book.
Are you asleep, a cigarette
between tight lips of earth and sky?

III. Mountain Rain

We wake before dawn to you tapping
on our tents. Knuckles of wet against canvas. You slip
inside our barely unzipped doors. We shrink
at your touch, forgetting we welcomed you
as guest by sleeping in a thin place.

IV. Spirit

I love what you weave too much.
I hang your tapestries
on the cold castle walls of my heart.
But you call me to love
your invisible hands. I am still

learning how to cherish what I cannot
touch.

GAUDETE

For Notre Dame

When I hear it in a carol or a chant I am
Reminded of its English offspring, *gaudy*.

Gaudy, like a chasuble stitched of proud silks
Sailed in from the Orient, like the diamond crust
Of an almost-ancient crucifix mounted on high,
Like woven array of a hundred voices raised
In the rood loft, the puffed chest of the ambulatory
And all its stalwart ribs standing guard over
The garden, g*audy.*

But *gaudete* is also the hair shirt, the candle stub,
The threadbare mantilla, the infant-cry in the narthex,
The catacombs' walls of soil, stone, bone.
Gaudete is the smoke-stained relic rescued
From fire, waiting in a dry, gray, dull vault
Somewhere in France, blessing the space with
Whatever moth and rust cannot destroy.

ENTANGLEMENT THEORY

or *What happened after with Antonia*

and then from four whole time zones away
you open your mouth and finish my sentence, and
only God gets to hear the whole thing,
from first capital letter to final period.

Who would've believed that your spirit could catch my meaning
midair like a baseball player and hold it fast, and find its finish?

Don't worry, you said once;
don't worry that you're going far away.
We don't need the railroad to string us together.
But those tight muscles in my forehead held onto you anyway,
never once pulling you nearer.
And then a year. And then a few more years.

And meanwhile, back on the other side of the country,
your children who hadn't met me yet
were the only ones who really knew me.
You said it was the photographs, your stories—
long lines of track laid from mind to mind,
crossing state lines, rivers, prairies, wives, and wars.

Please, help me remember.
If I start the question, even if it never gets answered,

will you finish it for me?

A YOUNG HUMMINGBIRD

A young hummingbird approaches my feeder,
Wings a flash of anxious silver,
Grimly eyeing me, the giver
Of the gift of glinting nectar.

Head aswivel, tensely twitching,
Guarding his own greedy sipping,
As if worried, maybe wondering
When I'll snatch back all he's loving.

Frantic bird with frantic trill,
Ever-moving, ever-shrill,
Maybe someday we both will
Know the space of Peace, Be Still.

MANHATTAN

In Midtown, massive cavern of my youth,
Skyscrapers flashed with phantoms of the truth,
All screens and sun-shadows along the walls
On either side like brick and metal jaws.
Within it rushed the world, in shoes and buses,
Fodder for New York's never-sated trusses,
And deeper still, the groaning gut of train
Twisted inside its middle like a chain.

We took that train each Monday. You were eight,
And danced effortlessly over curb and grate
And didn't know what half the ads were saying.
The city couldn't comprehend your playing.
And when the weather got crueler and colder
You sat there with me, ear upon my shoulder,
And round us roared the city, like a storm.
The earth cried out. Something was being born.

PUPILS

The tunnel with light at both ends:
The joy of and the fear of
Looking into it honestly
And saying just what you mean,
A sometimes-shuttered window, yawning
Often in the dark, tightening in brightness,
A circle, a space,
The soul of a face,
A student.

A student.
The soul of a face,
A circle, a space,
Often in the dark, tightening in brightness,
A sometimes-shuttered window, yawning
And saying just what you mean,
Looking into it honestly,
The joy of and the fear of
The tunnel with light at both ends.

PLANE GOD

Wrapped deep in the embrace of this plane, we rise
Through a thrashing thunderstorm, through gods

Of gray thunder and a cold, cursed rain
We rise, wrapped deep in the embrace of this plane,
We tear through the veil of violent wind, above, above,

Until all its swirling glory rests small as a footstool
Under our feet. Above the Rockies we rise,
Leaving the snowcaps behind in a streak of seconds,
Plowing toward the wild, we rise.

Threads of suburban streetlights glint below
Like eyes watching our massive ascension into
This wind-wrought, storm-torn sky-road on which we
Somehow safely roar, helpless in this deep
Airplane embrace, powerless in this great
Powerfulness, small in this hugeness, we
Sit still inside this speed. This rising is
A song my lungs are too feeble to sing,
A dance my legs are not nimble enough to learn.
This rising is not us, us small layfolk
Who wait in this silent, sterile sheath of
A plane, all earth a cold chaos outside.
Later, if we hatch from this square foot of
Space, will we flee from this great hug, reach out

Our own arms, and attempt to rise?

SONNET BY THOSE WHO STAY BEHIND

I'll see you again in many days, or a few.
Just leave your echo here within these walls
To wait in corners with your old footballs
And piles of papers, artifacts of you,
Reminding those remaining what is true
Behind the curtain every time it falls:
Choirs wait in quietness, till the calls
Of trumpets reunite them at their cue.
Till, then, dear friend, I ask you, leave your echo
For me to gather up while you are gone,
Like wildflowers, or penny after penny
Into a jar of moments I won't let go
Of till again you fill this room with song.
I'll see you again in a few days, or many.

III. NAVE

POETRY AND POSTULANCY

We are not all meant for meter, she says.
Still, you try on order like a vestment;
Long, sober, and reliable, it fits,
Or doesn't—it maddens you like slant rhyme,
Like prayers that impossibly find a home
Inside the swollen hours of weekdays.

This liturgy is both suitor and friend—
You wish and don't wish she'll stay on your mind,
This almost-lover, so completely wrong
For you, or not, but always somewhere near,
To taunt you with potential steadiness.
We are not all meant for meter, she says.

Perhaps you'll drop this habit and you'll run.
Still, we all marry something, or someone.

TO A CUTTER, AGE 14

Yesterday during the hike you jumped too far
and skinned your knee on a rock.
It might scar like my knee did
when I was young like you,
making a jagged island of white above the patella.

Yesterday during the hike I also jumped too far
and skinned my arm on a rock. I forgot about it,
until this morning when I rolled over
and felt it burning. Imagine my surprise
when I checked it,
and my forearm looked like yours.
It felt odd to see those familiar angry gashes
on my own skin.

When you saw my cuts yesterday your hand reached out
and touched my arm
and for one second your voice softened,
your eyes looked parent-like.

Interesting, isn't it, the earth chose for us
to bear one another's scars?
I think of Saint Francis,
whose hands and feet ran rivers of blood
as he limped down the mountain.

UNTANGLING

The mother finds joy in untangling
The necklaces. She pulls the silver strands,
Unbraiding gently, as if it is her
Young daughter's hair after a day
Outdoors. Time is of little importance:
For hours she untwists, a bold patience
In her fingers, fanning a fountain of
Graceful glittering loops. I watch her now,
Mirroring all her moves. It isn't me,
She says, pulling another necklace free.
They're made like this, to rest on collarbones
And hearts. They twist along the way. I nod,
Fingering my own around my neck, and
Reach to help. There is still more to undo.

CLOUDS

Somewhere north of the valley
the great sheet of the sky gathers unmade. Billows
of linen tumble over linen and
sing praises of mornings too frantic to
spend smoothing. It's as if the saints rolled
over and realized that it was an hour
later than they thought, with just enough time to make it without
    being actually late, so they leapt, like children, through the
    bedroom of the heavens, tossing aside cumulous pillows into
    corners for all the laymen below to see.

There's only ever just enough time;
not that we need to rush, you see—
we think we can start early, plot all our moves, but
in the end the bell of the sun rings bright and we know
that Providence knew
the whole time
that the heavens must be flung
in a white pile
to sooth the so-called ordered earth.

EPIPHANY

Sometimes when the moon swells
And glows on the edge of the ridge,
Sometimes when certain stars
Slip back into view with the winter,
Sometimes on nights when the planets
Beam brighter to us, I wonder,
What language does the sky speak?

I place my finger into the Pleiades.
I am a schoolchild following big letters
Across your page. I touch each point of light
Like it's a wound. I play connect-the-dots
With your celestial giants, make child-pictures
Out of speckles, each larger than our earth.

Carry me in your pocket across the desert.
Drop me at your doorstep someday
So I may offer you this gift of my reading.

THE ART OF LOVING

The art of loving might look like a bard's
Familiar ballad, playful yet precise—
All fingers dancing, never strained by self
Or hesitation, fret to joyful fret,
A perfect, reckless, troubadour's delight,
Like friends who wonder at the firmament's
Vast steadiness, how it remains the same,
Yet never ceases to draw our eyes up.

But I remember on too many days
The tremor of a grip too tight, the sound
Of hollow distance, the furrow of fear.

Release and practice, practice and release—
Until the dance of my hand moves within
A Spirit wiser than my mortal reach.

LITURGY

A man wearing knee braces walks laps
Around the Abbey of Gethsemani parking lot.
His gray hair is pulled back in a knot. He pumps
His arms crookedly to balance on his twisted legs.
I have seen him pass me like the second hand
Of a clock five or six times now. In the nearby
Tree, fragile sparrows sing vespers. The statue

On the hill watches with silent eyes. The man
Limps around again. No, not *limps*, his laps
Are too noble to be called *limps*. His baseball
Cap's blue brim half-covers his face. I try
Not to look too long at him for fear of being
Noticed, for fear of my admiration being
Mistaken for a baser fascination.

Like a prayer he circles steadily, and although his
Pain is present, it is not at the center of his step.

BIRD, GIFT

You hold the bird with open hands
Until it flies to distant lands.
You love when it returns again,
Within your palm, you see it then,
But if you try to tightly grasp
This gift, embrace it, hold it fast,
You lose it by its being too near—
By being free, it is more dear.

By being free, it is more dear.
You lose it by its being too near—
This gift, embrace it, hold it fast,
But if you try to tightly grasp
Within your palm, you see it then,
You love when it returns again,
Until it flies to distant lands.
You hold the bird with open hands.

TYPESETTING

It took four hours to print one sonnet.
I sat on a stool, picked eighteen-point
Baskerville out of a drawer for you;
You lined them up, backward and upside-down,
Until my poem, every tiny word,
Was re-written in metal, sheets, and ink.
We smell the page, admire our handiwork,
Then look with grave amusement at the clock.

This took longer to print than to write, I
Said to you with incredulity—
And then, a twinge of guilt, as if the speed
Of my pen was somehow superior
To this big, slow, precise, old-fashioned thing
We used to make my poem new again.

CURSIVE

In the beginning was one word,
A word continuous and full,
A single thread of ink, I've heard,
Who speaks in darkness, makes us whole.

A word continuous and ful-
Ly good, unlike our fractured lines,
Will speak in darkness, make us whole,
Piecemeal to peace, an act divine-

Ly good, unlike our fractured lines,
Which pop staccato with our fears.
Piecemeal to peace! An act divine
Will someday reconnect our years

Which pop staccato with our fears.
O longest line the light once drew,
Will someday you connect our years?
Will all that's broken be made new?

The longest line the light once drew
Will in the end still be one word,
And all that's broken may be new,
A single thread of ink, I've heard.

ENTERTAINING

What do God's people look like? she asks us during dinner.
She is fresh off a Greyhound from Baltimore,
jobless, homeless, and now sitting at my neighbor's table,
which is spread with meat and wine.
She is thin but she wears a queenly head wrap.
I think of Odysseus stumbling out of the bushes,
hair matted with leaves and sea-salt,
hands of a once-king begging for alms, for arms, for conveyance.
Full now, I wait for someone else to answer the question.

She spoons leftover salad into a Tupperware and answers it
    herself:
if you ask children what God's people look like,
they'll say they look like children.

I think back on the days I did the knocking, wind-tossed
with grimy guitar case in hand, kicked off sleet-soaked
boots and blessed houses with nothing but my need. I wonder
if our rags mask our riches, if when we
enter eager as street kids or washed-up sailors, we
grant open doors heavenly rewards.

SAINT JOSEPH

Down in the dust of the desert night
The father kneels, awake. His wife and child
Are still in sleep, wrapped in a holey shawl
Of humble wool, in fugitive slumber.
The sand blows sharp into Joseph's raised eyes.
He squints into his frail and furtive vigil,
Which stretches from this ground far into Egypt.

The weakest of the three must guard what's pure,
And tuck the blanket underneath their chins
And lead the ass across the anxious path
To carry them into their rest again.
He looks up, looks down. Prays. What's done is done:
A hail to his gently breathing wife,
A thank you to the heart of sleeping son.

BAREFOOT AT LOW TIDE,
KENNEBUNKPORT, MAINE

To walk through the mud flats, you must walk slow.
I grasp at your elbow, keep my head bowed low
To skim the silt, so soaked in ancient life
I nearly hear crustaceans cry out, like
Mountains, but hidden, smaller, older, still
On the outside, inside a magma, spill-
ing a little out the edges, eager
To make the earth more fecund, fresh, warmer
With their oyster-weight. My soles touch their shells
And silvery mud ribbons between my toes
As we step slow, ankle-deep in the slime,
Like creatures coalescing back in time,
Pulled gently to wet dust from which we came,
Before dry land, before things had a name.

ASH WEDNESDAY IN MAUI

Dust rises in corners where birds take off and land,
Dust rises inside blue-clear crests of waves breaking,
Dust rises from Dantean mountains crowned with fire—
How is an island this alive made of dust?

Once upon a time the earth's belly rumbled
And up came fire and ash, up came this island.
She has borne queens and lepers, soldiers and whalers,
Strangers and spouses. She has borne those willing
To mount up on wings and find her.

Dig a hole under Jerusalem and journey past hell;
Find the trapdoor that turns you upside-down
Back to the stars; you'll find yourself here:
Land embraced by ocean, precious in its aloneness,
Bearing fruit and luring tourists who hunger to rise.

The dust has settled. We come here to sleep. We come
Here not to come home, but to find it, maybe up
In the mountains, maybe among the birdsong, maybe
Embraced in our beds rocked awake and asleep
By Our Lady the ocean, learning life again
By lying down and returning to dust.

CITY NAVE

Stand on your head. You'll see that she's a boat
Winding between the waves of wailing walls,
Careening through the rush of siren-calls,
A small ship on a violent ocean. Smote
By sea-wind, still unyielding, she's afloat,
And unabashed by bitter gales and galls
She sails through the city's shifting halls,
Unchanging nave, intimate, yet remote.

So swim along the sidewalk to her door;
Turn, tossed explorer, right-side up again.
This ancient, mighty haven, grim and good,
Drags in the drowning to her drier floor
And bears the wounded through her healing hold
And bids you drink the drink, and eat the food.

IV. ALTAR

ECLIPSE GLASSES

And then, the sun. It looks into my face,
A father's eye, full of pity and grace.
Flimsy as faith and dark as afterlife,
I bought this blindness so that I will see.

BE FRUITFUL AND MULTIPLY

So, what is fruit? A star upon a bough,
A drop of sweetness buried in a jungle
Of vines and thorns, the treasure in the tangle,
The pulsing life emerging from a vow,
The golden knowledge we cannot have now,
Walled-in and waiting, guarded by an angel,
A soft thing we can slice and toss and mangle,
A sleeping story tucked in by the plough.

The once-abundant oranges are green
And meager from the blight. We buy a tree
And plant it in the desert far away.
And as the earth grows more barren and mean
This sapling will belong to you and me,
And maybe will bear much for us someday.

TWO WAYS TO BE A FLAME

The flame in the little, squat glass
Is doing a perpetual jig
Like an unselfconscious young girl.
She scrunches and stretches and stands,
She bows and blesses the air
With busy child's hands.

I catch sight of her from across the room
And accidentally smile. The small holy
Fool will draw others into her happy
Flicker until all of her fuel runs out.

The taper's flame
Points, icon-like,
So still. She stands
In her white robe
Which runs in tiers
Over a straight
Spine, a tall spire.
A mandorla
Glows motionless
Behind her face.

I make eye contact with her 'cross the room
And stop all that I'm doing, save slow breaths.
She will be a beacon until the day
She touches earth again in grace-filled gray.

TRAPPIST ABBEY AFTER RAIN

The earth is bursting with insect-joy.
They shoot up from the grass around my feet
Like miniature fireworks when I walk through,
Rockets of orange and yellow and blue,
Ladybugs, butterflies, crickets, all the
Bugs that children's books are written about
Click and whir and rat-a-tat and hum
In flashing festival around the cloister.
My silence bade this celebration sound
Loud enough for my oft-distracted ear,
Which, when at rest, is finally generous,
And welcomes all the poor I never hear,
The lowly ones of antenna and wing,
Who, in their smallness, still know how to sing.

PROMISED LANDS

Piano through the screen door, hushing wind
In palms and orange blossoms, bringing breath
Of bloom onto our dusty porch. I sit
And wonder at the kindness of Phoenix,
Oasis-city stretching peak to peak
Between the brown and brown, the dead and dead—

And yet I know that in that ragged beyond
Deep streams are hidden, cold and clean to drink,
And craggy plants birth fringes of golden flowers,
And skies will surprise with gifts of rain.
And so the earth is only made for life,
For life is all there is, all that can be.
No matter how dry its corners, in the heart
God springs the fountain. Will we come to see?

VOLLEYBALL

or Of the high school athletes who preferred form to free verse

The players love the net. They raise it high
Like heraldry in the gymnasium,
Unfurl it edge to edge, a standard set,
A boundary for their bounding, bruising play.
A battle line drawn firmly in the earth,
The net expects a leap and a long reach;
The players reverently touch its stern face
At every spike; it flutters, unperturbed.
The net conducts their dance. The back-and-forth,
The contra and the canter to the line,
The gentle set and death-defying dive,
The meeting, parting, serving, sprinting. Then
After the game, they show me all their wounds.
No glory, they say, if not for the net.

TURBULENCE

My student's plane crashed in the snow.
I never quite know how to pray
For the dead. But I often try.
To God, I say,

My student's plane crashed. In the snow
The wings looked brittle, like a bird's.
And the photograph was so small.
It looked absurd,

My student's plane. Crashed in the snow
She cannot tell us why she fell.
I keep the note she wrote in class
Like it can tell

My students. Planes crash in the snow
Most every year. I cross my heart
And hope to live. The engine sings
As we depart.

My student's plane crashed in the snow.
I see her, sometimes, in the sky,
A genuflect of silver wings
Still crossing by.

BUYING A HOUSE ON THE FEAST OF SAINT FRANCIS

He sells the final book. His shelves are bare.
He puts the gold into the leper's hand.
His parents rage. He strips his robes and says
He cannot care. He walks away to hug
The sick. There is laughter. He owns nothing,
Everything. He is so far from God that
He has found him. He will wander the earth
Until death. He knows that to love a thing
It cannot be his. He knows to love a
Thing it must all be home.

We will combine our books and organize
Them into genres alphabetically.
We'll sign shadows of paperwork on screens.
We will lose cash and gain equity. Our
Parents will applaud. We will park our cars
Like conquistadors on our purchased shore
And yank the SOLD sign out like a weak tree.
We will own everything, nothing. We will
Be close enough to our jobs to get by.
We will call a piece of earth our own. We
Will know that for a thing to be ours we
Cannot love it too much. We will know to
Be home in a thing, it must all be love.

www.ingramcontent.com/pod-product-compliance
Lightning Source LLC
Chambersburg PA
CBHW060420050426
42449CB00009B/2044